INSPIRED WORDS OF EDIFICATION

"Inspirational Empowerment"

Let every one of us please his neighbour for his good and edification (Romans 15:2).

~Pastor Flora M Skipwith~

ISPIRED WORDS OF EDIFICATION

Copyright @ 2018 Word of Reconciliation Restoration Outreach Ministries Inc.

Unless otherwise noted, Scripture quotations are taken from the Holy Bible, King James Version.

All rights reserved. No part of this publication may be reproduced, stored in a retrieval system, or transmitted in any form by means electronic, mechanical, photocopying, recording or otherwise, without prior permission in writing from the publisher.

Special Acknowledgements

First and foremost, I give all honor and glory to my Lord and Savior Jesus Christ who is my **Strong Tower**, my **ALL** and **ALL**. He's the **Author** and **Finisher** of my faith, the one who always gives me the desires of my heart. The Lord has made my hands fruitful and blessed the works of my hand!

I must also take this time to make known and honor publicly, my friend, my heart beat, my husband Bishop Dexter T Skipwith who is Co-founder at Word of Reconciliation Restoration Outreach Ministries. I Thank you for always encouraging me, you're my number one supporter with the vision. I just want you to know that the Lord have used you tremendously to be the wind at my back each time He pressed upon my spirit to step out in faith.

Special Acknowledgements

To my children, their children, and their children's children. I assure you when God is for you, it's more than the whole world against you. Always allow the Lord to be your guiding factor; and delight yourself in him. He will give you the desires of your heart. NEVER FORGET YOUR GOD: THE LORD JESUS CHRIST!!!

     I also want to give special thanks to each and every one of you for supporting this launch for the work of the ministry. This is the beginning of my publication, and I trust in the Lord that my words of edification and exhortation with biblical confirmation will bless you divinely!

                      Grace & Peace Be Multiplied,

PREFACE

This book contains inspired words of edification that I spoke while meditating and examining myself to see whether or not I'm abiding in the faith. For faith cometh by hearing, and hearing is by the Word of God that must be applicable in our daily living to be effective. There are also scriptures included for instruction in righteousness.

The purpose of this book is to edify the believer in the faith. This book is designed for believers of like precious faith, and is highly recommend for new converts and layman's. This book can be used as an aid in the renewing of the mind daily.

For we are to exhort one another daily, while it is called Today; lest any of you be hardened through the deceitfulness of sin (Hebrews 3:13).

All scripture is given by inspiration of God, and is profitable for doctrine, for reproof, for correction, for instruction in righteousness (2 Timothy 3:16).

"And now I commend you to God and to the word of His grace, which is able to build you up and to give you the inheritance among all those who are sanctified.(Acts 20:32).

POSITIONALLY WE ARE ALREADY SEATED IN CHRIST: SO WE CAN WALK OUT OUR HEAVENLY POSITION IN THE EARTH AS IT ALREADY IS IN THE HEAVENLY!

And hath raised us up together, and made us sit together in heavenly places in Christ Jesus: (Ephesians 2:6).

As ye have therefore received Christ Jesus the Lord, so walk ye in him: Rooted and built up in him, and stablished in the faith, as ye have been taught, abounding therein with thanksgiving (Colossians 2:6-7).

*When you're born again, your thoughts become God's thoughts when renewing your mind daily with His Word, and your ways become God's ways when led by His Spirit. For as many as are led by the Spirit of God are the sons of God: And he that is joined unto the Lord is one Spirit, you are ONE in Him!

DO NOT ALLOW ANYONE SAVED OR UNSAVED IMPRISON YOUR MIND BY SPEAKING WORDS TO YOU THAT ARE CONTRARY TO WHAT GOD HAS ALREADY SAID ABOUT YOU:

For as he thinketh in his heart, so is he: Eat and drink, saith he to thee; but his heart is not with thee (Proverbs 23:7).

"What shall we then say to these things? If God *be* for us, who *can be* against us?" Who shall lay any thing to the charge of God's elect? *It is* God that justifieth. Who *is* he that condemneth? *It is* Christ that died, yea rather, that is risen again, who is even at the right hand of God, who also maketh intercession for us. (Romans 8:31, 33-34).

SPIRITUALLY YOU ARE IN THE WRONG MARRIAGE COVENANT IF YOU'RE NOT IN COVENTANT WITH CHRIST: IT'S TIME FOR A NAME CHANGE!

For this cause I bow my knees unto the Father of our Lord Jesus Christ, Of whom the whole family in heaven and earth is named (Ephesians 3:14-15).

Neither is there salvation in any other: for there is none other name under heaven given among men, whereby we must be saved (Acts 4:12).

That at the name of Jesus every knee should bow, of things in heaven, and things in earth, and things under the earth; And that every tongue should confess that Jesus Christ is Lord, to the glory of God the Father (Philippians 2:10-11).

GOD'S AMAZING GRACE HAVE EQUIPPED US TO ENDURE THIS RACE OF FAITH THAT'S SET BEFORE US:

Looking unto Jesus the author and finisher of our faith; who for the joy that was set before him endured the cross, despising the shame, and is set down at the right hand of the throne of God (Hebrews 12:2).

Who hath saved us, and called *us* with an holy calling, not according to our works, but according to his own purpose and grace, which was given us in Christ Jesus before the world began, (2 Timothy 1:9).

THE VERY THING SATAN HAS ALWAYS ATTEPTED TO USE FOR BAIT, "WHICH IS WOMAN!" GOD'S GRACE HAVE CALLED AND MADE GREAT:

"Favour *is* deceitful, and beauty *is* vain: *but* a woman *that* feareth the LORD, she shall be praised (Proverbs 31:30)."

A gracious woman retaineth honour: and strong men retain riches (Proverbs 11:16).

There is neither Jew nor Greek, there is neither bond nor free, there is neither *male* nor *female*: for ye are all *one* in Christ Jesus (Galatians 3:28).

ARE YOU REIGNING OR RUNNING? NO MORE RUNNING: FOR THE GODLY SHALL BE PERSECUTED AND THE RIGHTEOUS SHALL HAVE MANY AFFLICTIONS. ARE YOU SUFFERING? BE OF GOOD COURAGE IT'S FOR HIS NAME SAKE:

If we suffer, we shall also reign with him: if we deny him, he also will deny us (2 Timothy 2:12).

But and if ye suffer for righteousness' sake, happy are ye: and be not afraid of their terror, neither be troubled (1 Peter 3:14).

For unto you it is given in the behalf of Christ, not only to believe on him, but also to suffer for his sake; (Philippians 1:29).

THE WORD OF GOD IS SOUND DOCTRINE: IT WILL GIVE YOU SOUNDNESS OF MIND AND KEEP YOU FROM BEING TOSSED TO AND FRO. IT'S AN ANCHOR FOR YOUR SOUL!

For God hath not given us the spirit of fear; but of power, and of love, and of a sound mind (2 Timothy 1:7).

Wherefore lay apart all filthiness and superfluity of naughtiness, and receive with meekness the engrafted word, which is able to save your souls (James 1:21).

Which *hope* we have as an anchor of the soul, both sure and stedfast, and which entereth into that within the veil; (Hebrews 6:19).

CONTINUE TO PRAY: YOUR PRAYERS ARE EFFECTIVE AND GOD'S EARS ARE ATTENTIVE!

And if we know that he hear us, whatsoever we ask, we know that we have the petitions that we desired of him (1 John 5:15).

For the eyes of the Lord are over the righteous, and his ears are open unto their prayers: but the face of the Lord is against them that do evil (1Peter 3:12).

MONDAY'S ARE NOT FOR MOURNING ARE MURMURING: SO OPEN YOUR MOUTH AND GIVE GOD THANKS!

This is the day which the LORD hath made; we will rejoice and be glad in it (Psalm 118:24).

In everything give thanks: for this is the will of God in Christ Jesus concerning you (1 Thessalonians 5:18).

By him therefore let us offer the sacrifice of praise to God continually, that is, the fruit of our lips giving thanks to his name (Hebrews 13:15).

GOD IS NOT A GOD WHO SLEEPS NOR SLUMBER: HE HEARS, HE SEES, HE KNOWS. AND WHEN YOU CALL UPON HIM, HE WILL ANSWER YOU. SO BE NOT DISMAYED FOR HE IS FAITHFUL WHO PROMISED!

God is not a man, that he should lie; neither the son of man, that he should repent: hath he said, and shall he not do it? or hath he spoken, and shall he not make it good? (Numbers 23:19).

There hath no temptation taken you but such as is common to man: but God is faithful, who will not suffer you to be tempted above that ye are able; but will with the temptation also make a way to escape, that ye may be able to bear it (1 Corinthians 10:13).

A CHILD OF GOD IS NOT "A NOBODY TRYING TO TELL EVERYBODY:" THEY ARE SON'S OF GOD

Behold, what manner of love the Father hath bestowed upon us, that we should be called the sons of God: therefore the world knoweth us not, because it knew him not. Beloved, now are we the sons of God, and it doth not yet appear what we shall be: but we know that, when he shall appear, we shall be like him; for we shall see him as he is (1 John 3:1-2).

For we are his workmanship, created in Christ Jesus unto good works, which God hath before ordained that we should walk in them (Ephesians 2:10).

CELERBRATE JESUS IN THE MORNING, IN THE NOON DAY, IN THE EVENING: CELERBRATE JESUS ALL DAY LONG!!!

Wherefore God also hath highly exalted him, and given him a name which is above every name: That at the name of Jesus every knee should bow, of things in heaven, and things in earth, and things under the earth; And that every tongue should confess that Jesus Christ is Lord, to the glory of God the Father (Philippians 2:9-11).

WHAT SEEDS ARE YOU SOWING OUT OF YOUR MOUTH?

Death and life are in the power of the tongue: and they that love it shall eat the fruit thereof (Proverbs 18:21).

Be not deceived; God is not mocked: for whatsoever a man soweth, that shall he also reap (Galatians 6:7).

A good man out of the good treasure of his heart bringeth forth that which is good; and an evil man out of the evil treasure of his heart bringeth forth that which is evil: for of the abundance of the heart his mouth speaketh (Luke 6:45).

THERE'S A FULL BENEFIT PACKAGE INCLUDED IN YOUR SALVATION:

For in him dwelleth all the fulness of the Godhead bodily. And ye are complete in him, which is the head of all principality and power: (Colossians 2:9-10).

The blessing of the LORD, it maketh rich, and he addeth no sorrow with it (Proverbs 10:22).

Beloved, I wish above all things that thou mayest prosper and be in health, even as thy soul prospereth (3 John v 2).

GOD HAVE GIVEN ME A "LIFE SENTENCE" IN JESUS:

For the wages of sin is death; but the gift of God is eternal life through Jesus Christ our Lord (Romans 6:23).

And whosoever liveth and believeth in me shall never die. Believest thou this? (John 11:26).

For God sent not his Son into the world to condemn the world; but that the world through him might be saved (John 3:17).

ARE YOU CELERBRATING YOUR SPIRITUAL BIRTHDAY?

Of his own will begat he us with the word of truth, that we should be a kind of firstfruits of his creatures (James 1:18).

Being born again, not of corruptible seed, but of incorruptible, by the word of God, which liveth and abideth for ever (1 Peter 1:23).

Now this I say, brethren, that flesh and blood cannot inherit the kingdom of God; neither doth corruption inherit incorruption (1 Corinthians 15:50).

WHEN YOU EMBRACE YOUR CROSS, YOU'LL WEAR YOUR CROWN:

Then Jesus said to His disciples, "If anyone wishes to come after Me, he must deny himself, and take up his cross and follow Me. "For whoever wishes to save his life will lose it; but whoever loses his life for My sake will find it. "For what will it profit a man if he gains the whole world and forfeits his soul? Or what will a man give in exchange for his soul? (Matthew 16:24-26).

Blessed is the man that endureth temptation: for when he is tried, he shall receive the crown of life, which the Lord hath promised to them that love him (James 1:12).

DO NOT ALLOW ANYONE HOLD YOU PRISONER TO YOUR PAST: FOR GOD HAS GIVEN YOU A FUTURE!

Therefore if any man be in Christ, he is a new creature: old things are passed away; behold, all things are become new (2 Corinthians 5:17).

Brethren, I count not myself to have apprehended: but this one thing I do, forgetting those things which are behind, and reaching forth unto those things which are before, I press toward the mark for the prize of the high calling of God in Christ Jesus (Philippians 3:13-14).

Therefore we are buried with him by baptism into death: that like as Christ was raised up from the dead by the glory of the Father, even so we also should walk in newness of life (Romans 6:4).

HOW ARE YOU WALKING? IF YOU'RE WALKING BY WHAT YOU SEE IN THE NATURAL IT WILL DISAPPOINT YOU:

While we look not at the things which are seen, but at the things which are not seen: for the things which are seen are temporal; but the things which are not seen are eternal (2 Corinthians 4:18).

For we walk by faith, not by sight (2 Corinthians 5:7).

Beloved, now are we the sons of God, and it doth not yet appear what we shall be: but we know that, when he shall appear, we shall be like him; for we shall see him as he is. And every man that hath this hope in him purifieth himself, even as he is pure (1 John 3:2-3).

ALL THINGS ARE POSSIBLE TO THEM WHO'S TRUST IS IN GOD!

And Jesus said unto them, Because of your unbelief: for verily I say unto you, If ye have faith as a grain of mustard seed, ye shall say unto this mountain, Remove hence to yonder place; and it shall remove; and nothing shall be impossible unto you (Matthew 17:20).

For all the promises of God in Him are Yea, and in Him Amen, unto the glory of God by us (2 Corinthians 1:20).

YOU'RE LOOKING FOR LOVE IN ALL THE WRONG PLACES: LOVE BEGINS WITH GOD FIRST!

For God so loved the world, that he gave his only begotten Son, that whosoever believeth in him should not perish, but have everlasting life (John 3:16).

Greater love hath no man than this, that a man lay down his life for his friends (John 15:13).

But God, who is rich in mercy, for his great love wherewith he loved us, Even when we were dead in sins, hath quickened us together with Christ, by grace ye are saved (Ephesians 2:4-5).

YOU GOT BREATH? THAN PRAISE THE LORD!

Let everything that hath breath praise the LORD. Praise ye the LORD (Psalms 150:6).

But you are a chosen generation, a royal priesthood, a holy nation, a people for his own; that you should show forth the praises of him who has called you out of darkness into his marvelous light (1 Peter 2:9).

Rejoice in the LORD, O ye righteous: for praise is comely for the upright (Psalms 33:1).

HE WHOM JESUS HAVE FORGIVEN THE MOST, WILL LOVE HIM THE MOST!

Wherefore I say unto thee, Her sins, which are many, are forgiven; for she loved much: but to whom little is forgiven, *the same* loveth little. And he said unto her, Your sins are forgiven. (Luke 7:47-48).

My little children, these things write I unto you, that ye sin not. And if any man sin, we have an advocate with the Father, Jesus Christ the righteous: And he is the propitiation for our sins: and not for ours only, but also for the sins of the whole world (1 John 2:1-2).

*Oh how I love Jesus because he first loved me. He's sweet I know, He's sweet I know, and I'll tell the world wherever I go, that I have a Savior and He's sweet I know!!!!

STOP WORRYING ABOUT TOMORROW AND WHAT COULD HAPPEN TODAY: HAVE TRUST IN GOD, AND LET HIM LEAD YOU EVERY STEP OF THE WAY!

Therefore take no thought, saying, What shall we eat? or, What shall we drink? or, Wherewithal shall we be clothed? (For after all these things do the Gentiles seek:) for your heavenly Father knoweth that ye have need of all these things. But seek ye first the kingdom of God, and his righteousness; and all these things shall be added unto you (Matthew 6: 31-33).

"The steps of a *good* man are ordered by the LORD: and he delighteth in his way" (Psalms 37:23).

DO YOU HAVE THE HOLY GHOST SINCE YOU BELIEVED?

In whom ye also trusted, after that ye heard the word of truth, the gospel of your salvation: in whom also after that ye believed, ye were sealed with that holy Spirit of promise, Which is the earnest of our inheritance until the redemption of the purchased possession, unto the praise of his glory (Ephesians 1:13-14).

But ye shall receive power, after that the Holy Ghost is come upon you: and ye shall be witnesses unto me both in Jerusalem, and in all Judaea, and in Samaria, and unto the uttermost part of the earth (Acts 1:8).

A BELIEVER WHO IS MENTALLY DISTURBED, IS ONE WHO FAILS TO RENEW THEIR MIND WITH THE WORD OF GOD:

And be renewed in the spirit of your mind; And that ye put on the new man, which after God is created in righteousness and true holiness. (Ephesians 4:23-24).

I beseech you therefore, brethren, by the mercies of God, that ye present your bodies a living sacrifice, holy, acceptable unto God, which is your reasonable service. And be not conformed to this world: but be ye transformed by the renewing of your mind, that ye may prove what is that good, and acceptable, and perfect, will of God (Romans 12: 1-2).

WE ARE VICTORIOUS: OUR DAILY VICTORY IS MANIFESTED WHEN WE TRUST AND ACT UPON WHAT GOD SAID IN HIS WORD:

For whatsoever is born of God overcometh the world: and this is the victory that overcometh the world, even our faith (1 John 5:4).

But be ye doers of the word, and not hearers only, deceiving your own selves. For if any be a hearer of the word, and not a doer, he is like unto a man beholding his natural face in a glass: For he beholdeth himself, and goeth his way, and straightway forgetteth what manner of man he was. But whoso looketh into the perfect law of liberty, and continueth therein, he being not a forgetful hearer, but a doer of the work, this man shall be blessed in his deed (James 1:22-25).

INSPIRED WORDS OF EDIFICATION

WHEN YOU'RE BORN-AGAIN YOUR'RE NO LONGER A "SINNER SAVED BY GRACE": YOU'RE NOW A SAINT!

Giving thanks unto the Father, which hath made us meet to be partakers of the inheritance of the *saints* in light. Who hath delivered us from the power of darkness, and hath translated us into the kingdom of his dear Son: (Colossians 1:12-13).

ARE YOUR LIPS FRUITFUL UNTO GOD?

By him therefore let us offer the sacrifice of praise to God continually, that is, the fruit of our lips giving thanks to his name (Hebrews 13:15).

In every thing give thanks: for this is the will of God in Christ Jesus concerning you (1 Thessalonians 5:18).

YOU DON'T HAVE TO GO THROUGH LIFE COMFORTLESS!

I will not leave you comfortless: I will come to you. But the Comforter, which is the Holy Ghost, whom the Father will send in my name, he shall teach you all things, and bring all things to your remembrance, whatsoever I have said unto you. Peace I leave with you, my peace I give unto you: not as the world giveth, give I unto you. Let not your heart be troubled, neither let it be afraid. (John 14:18, 26-27).

Blessed *be* God, even the Father of our Lord Jesus Christ, the Father of mercies, and the God of all comfort. Who comforteth us in all our tribulation, that we may be able to comfort them which are in any trouble, by the comfort wherewith we ourselves are comforted of God (2 Corinthians 1:3-4).

LET IT GO! FORGIVE THEM OF THEIR TRESPASSES: FOR JESUS HAVE ALREADY PAID THE PRICE FOR IT!

But if ye forgive not men their trespasses, neither will your Father forgive your trespasses (Matthews 6:15).

"Forbearing one another, and forgiving one another, if any man have a quarrel against any: even as Christ forgave you, so also *do* ye" (Colossians 3:13).

Therefore if thine enemy hunger, feed him; if he thirst, give him drink: for in so doing thou shalt heap coals of fire on his head. Be not overcome of evil, but overcome evil with good (Romans 12:20-21).

KNOW THEM THAT LABOR AMONG YOU! FELLOWSHIP WITH A LIBERATOR NOT A LEGALIST: FOR A LEGALIST WILL IMPART CONDEMNATION & DEATH, BUT A LIBERATOR IMPARTS LIBERTY & LIFE!

Beware of dogs, beware of evil workers, beware of the concision. For we are the circumcision, which worship God in the spirit, and rejoice in Christ Jesus, and have no confidence in the flesh (Philippians 3:2-3).

There is therefore now no condemnation to them which are in Christ Jesus, who walk not after the flesh, but after the Spirit. For the law of the Spirit of life in Christ Jesus hath made me free from the law of sin and death (Romans 8:1-2).

A SPIRITUAL BATH IS NEEDED DAILY: ALLOW THE WORD OF GOD TO WASH YOU. THE LORD JESUS CHRIST IS WAITING TO CLEANSE YOU!

If we confess our sins, he is faithful and just to forgive us our sins, and to cleanse us from all unrighteousness (1 John 1:9).

That he might sanctify and cleanse it with the washing of water by the word. That he might present it to himself a glorious church, not having spot, or wrinkle, or any such thing; but that it should be holy and without blemish (Ephesians 5:26-27).

THE LIFE OF A BELIEVER IS A WAY OF SELF DENIAL: HAVING NO DESIRE TO GLORY IN THE FLESH TO MAKE IT ABOUT ONE'S SELF (me, myself, and I)!

And they that are Christ's have crucified the flesh with the affections and lusts (Galatians 5:24).

But God forbid that I should glory, save in the cross of our Lord Jesus Christ, by whom the world is crucified unto me, and I unto the world (Galatians 6:14).

And he said to them all, If any man will come after me, let him deny himself, and take up his cross daily, and follow me (Luke 9:23).

LOVE IS NOT A FOUR LETTER WORD: IT'S A LIFE, AND THE LIFE IS THE LIGHT OF MEN!

Hereby perceive we the love of God, because he laid down his life for us: and we ought to lay down our lives for the brethren (1 John 3:16).

Love worketh no ill to his neighbor: therefore love is the fulfilling of the law (Romans 13:10).

And above all things have fervent charity among yourselves: for charity shall cover the multitude of sins (1 Peter 4:8).

A CHILD OF GOD CAN CELERBRATE INDEPENDENCE DAY EVERY DAY!

Stand fast therefore in the liberty wherewith Christ hath made us free, and be not entangled again with the yoke of bondage. Behold, I Paul say unto you, that if ye be circumcised, Christ shall profit you nothing. For I testify again to every man that is circumcised, that he is a debtor to do the whole law. Christ is become of no effect unto you, whosoever of you are justified by the law; ye are fallen from grace (Galatians 5:1-4).

And ye shall know the truth, and the truth shall make you free. If the Son therefore shall make you free, ye shall be free indeed (John 8:32, 36).

THE WORD OF GOD IS LIKEN UNTO A FULL LENGTH MIRROR: WE CAN SEE HOW DRESSED WE ARE WHEN WE PUT ON CHRIST OR HOW NAKED WE ARE WITHOUT HIM!

And that ye put on the new man, which after God is created in righteousness and true holiness (Ephesians 4:24).

For if anyone be a hearer of the word, and not a doer, he is like unto a man beholding his natural face in a glass: For he beholdeth himself, and goeth his way, and straight forgetteth what manner of man he was (James1:23-24).

WHY ARE YOU STILL LOOKING FOR JESUS' FOOTPRINTS?

As ye have therefore received Christ Jesus the Lord, so walk ye in him (Colossians 2:6).

He that saith he abideth in him ought himself also so to walk, even as he walked (1 John 2:6).

HOW COULD YOU? WHY SHOULD YOU STRESS WHEN GOD HAS SACRIFICED HIS VERY BEST SO WE CAN ENTER INTO HIS REST!

Come unto me, all ye that labour and are heavy laden, and I will give you rest. Take my yoke upon you, and learn of me; for I am meek and lowly in heart: and ye shall find rest unto your souls (Matthews 11:28-29).

A CLICHE: "AN EMPTY WAGON MAKES THE MOST NOISE" THANKS BE UNTO GOD FOR BEING LIKEN UNTO AN EMPTY WAGON WITHOUT THE HEAVY LOAD:

Casting all your care upon him; for he careth for you (1Peter 5:7).

Make a joyful noise unto the LORD, all the earth: *make a loud noise*, and rejoice, and sing praise (Psalms 98:4).

DIDN'T YOU KNOW OUR AFFLICTIONS, PERSUCUTIONS, AND SUFFERINGS ARE A PART OF OUR SPIRITUAL GROWTH?

For our light affliction, which is but for a moment, worketh for us a far more exceeding and eternal weight of glory (2 Corinthians 4:17).

Yea, and all that will live godly in Christ Jesus shall suffer persecution (2 Timothy 3:12).

For unto you it is given in the behalf of Christ, not only to believe on him, but also to suffer for his sake (Philippians 1:29).

OUR WORDS SHOULD NEVER "ATTACT" BUT "ATTRACT", EVEN IN CHASTENING:

Brethren, if a man be overtaken in a fault, ye which are spiritual, restore such an one in the spirit of meekness; considering thyself, lest thou also be tempted (Ephesians 6:1).

"Let no corrupt communication proceed out of your mouth, but that which is good to the use of edifying, that it may minister grace unto the hearers" (Ephesians 4:29).

A soft answer turneth away wrath: but grievous words stir up anger (Proverbs 15:1).

DON'T BE A PASSIVE BELIEVER:

Therefore to him that knoweth to do good, and doeth it not, to him it is sin (James 4:17).

Lay hands suddenly on no man, neither be partaker of other men's sins: keep thyself pure (1 Timothy 5:22).

Let no man deceive you with vain words: for because of these things cometh the wrath of God upon the children of disobedience. Be not ye therefore partakers with them. For ye were sometimes darkness, but now are ye light in the Lord: walk as children of light: (For the fruit of the Spirit is in all goodness and righteousness and truth; (Ephesians 5:6-9).

HAVE YOUR LOVING KINDNESS BEEN TAKEN FOR WEAKNESS?

And be ye kind one to another, tenderhearted, forgiving one another, even as God for Christ's sake hath forgiven you (Ephesians 4:32).

The LORD hath appeared of old unto me, saying, Yea, I have loved thee with an everlasting love: therefore with loving kindness have I drawn thee (Jeremiah 31:3).

DON'T ALLOW THE CIRCUMSTANCES OF LIFE CAUSE YOU TO MOVE AHEAD OF GOD PREMATURELY AND ABORT; OR GIVE PREMATURE BIRTH TO GOD'S PURPOSE AND PLAN FOR YOUR LIFE!

For I know the thoughts that I think toward you, saith the LORD, thoughts of peace, and not of evil, to give you an expected end (Jeremiah 29:11).

Every man's work shall be made manifest: for the day shall declare it, because it shall be revealed by fire; and the fire shall try every man's work of what sort it is. If any man's work abide which he hath built thereupon, he shall receive a reward. If any man's work shall be burned, he shall suffer loss: but he himself shall be saved; yet so as by fire (1 Corinthians 3:13-15).

WE COULD NEVER LOVE GOD ON OUR OWN EVEN IF WE WANTED TO:

We love him, because he first loved us (1 John 4:19).

Even when we were dead in sins, hath quickened us together with Christ, (by grace ye are saved;) And hath raised us up together, and made us sit together in heavenly places in Christ Jesus: That in the ages to come he might shew the exceeding riches of his grace in his kindness toward us through Christ Jesus. For by grace are ye saved through faith; and that not of yourselves: it is the gift of God: Not of works, lest any man should boast (Ephesians 2:5-9).

DO YOU WANT TO BE MADE WHOLE?

Beware lest any man spoil you through philosophy and vain deceit, after the tradition of men, after the rudiments of the world, and not after Christ. For in him dwelleth all the fulness of the Godhead bodily. And ye are complete in him, which is the head of all principality and power (Ephesians 2:8-10).

I am the vine, ye are the branches: He that abideth in me, and I in him, the same bringeth forth much fruit: for without me ye can do nothing (John 15:5).

When Jesus saw him lie, and knew that he had been now a long time in that case, he saith unto him, Wilt thou be made whole? (John 5:6).

DO YOU WANT TO BE MADE WHOLE?

And he said unto her, Daughter, thy faith hath made thee whole; go in peace, and be whole of thy plague (Mark 5:34).

If ye abide in me, and my words abide in you, ye shall ask what ye will, and it shall be done unto you (John 15:7).

WHY ARE YOU GOING FROM PLACE TO PLACE LOOKING FOR SIGNS AND WONDERS: ARE YOU A BELIEVER?

And these signs shall follow them that believe; In my name shall they cast out devils; they shall speak with new tongues; They shall take up serpents; and if they drink any deadly thing, it shall not hurt them; they shall lay hands on the sick, and they shall recover (Mark 16:17-18).

Now unto him that is able to do exceeding abundantly above all that we ask or think, according to the power that worketh in us (Ephesians 3:20).

EDIFYING THINGS TO THINK ON!

Finally, brethren, whatsoever things are true, whatsoever things are honest, whatsoever things are just, whatsoever things are pure, whatsoever things are lovely, whatsoever things are of good report; if there be any virtue, and if there be any praise, think on these things (Philippians 4:8).

Thou wilt keep him in perfect peace, whose mind is stayed on thee: because he trusteth in thee (Isaiah 26:3).

ARE YOU WATCHING AND WAITHING FOR JESUS' RETURN?

But of the times and the seasons, brethren, ye have no need that I write unto you. For yourselves know perfectly that the day of the Lord so cometh as a thief in the night. For when they shall say, Peace and safety; then sudden destruction cometh upon them, as travail upon a woman with child; and they shall not escape. But ye, brethren, are not in darkness, that that day should overtake you as a thief. Ye are all the children of light, and the children of the day: we are not of the night, nor of darkness (1Thessalonians 5:1-5).

EVERY DAY WITH JESUS IS SWEETER THAN THE DAY BEFORE: HE IS THE LOVER OF MY SOUL !

For to me to live *is* Christ, and to die *is* gain (Philippians 1:21).

I am crucified with Christ: nevertheless I live; yet not I, but Christ liveth in me: and the life which I now live in the flesh I live by the faith of the Son of God, who loved me, and gave himself for me (Galatians 2:20).

YOU CAN FIND REST AT HOLY GHOST RESORT!

There remaineth therefore a rest to the people of God. For he that is entered into his rest, he also hath ceased from his own works, as God did from his (Hebrews 4:9-10).

WHEN YOU'RE BORN-AGAIN, YOU ARE NO LONGER CONSIDERED AN OFFSPRING OF GOD: YOU'RE NOW THE SONS & DAUGHTERS OF GOD:

Behold, what manner of love the Father hath bestowed upon us, that we should be called the sons of God: therefore the world knoweth us not, because it knew him not. Beloved, now are we the sons of God, and it doth not yet appear what we shall be: but we know that, when he shall appear, we shall be like him; for we shall see him as he is. And every man that hath this hope in him purifieth himself, even as he is pure (1 John 3:1-3).

Be ye therefore followers of God, as dear children; (Ephesians 5:1).

FAITH IS TRUSTING WITHOUT SEEING, FOR BELIEF IS OF THE HEART: THEREFORE SPEAK AND YOU SHALL RECEIVE HOW YOU BELIEVE!

Jesus saith unto him, Thomas, because thou hast seen me, thou hast believed: blessed are they that have not seen, and yet have believed (John 20:29).

Therefore I say unto you, What things soever ye desire, when ye pray, believe that ye receive *them*, and ye shall have *them* (Mark 11:24).

COMPELLED v COMPETITIVE: EVERY STAR HAS IT'S OWN GLORY. SO THERE IS NO NEED TO COMPETE, JUST LET YOUR LIGHT SHINE!

Let your light so shine before men, that they may see your good works, and glorify your Father which is in heaven (Matthew 5:16).

For I say, through the grace given unto me, to every man that is among you, not to think *of himself* more highly than he ought to think; but to think soberly, according as God hath dealt to every man the measure of faith For just as each of us has one body with many members, and these members do not all have the same function, So we, *being* many, are one body in Christ, and every one members one of another. (Romans 12:3-5).

OUR PAST LIFE IS LIKENED UNTO THE OLD TESTAMENT! IT'S FOR OUR TEACHING. OUR NEW LIFE IS NEW TESTAMENT, WE ARE NOW LIVING EPISTLES:

Do we begin again to commend ourselves? or need we, as some others, epistles of commendation to you, or letters of commendation from you? Ye are our epistle written in our hearts, known and read of all men: Forasmuch as ye are manifestly declared to be the epistle of Christ ministered by us, written not with ink, but with the Spirit of the living God; not in tables of stone, but in fleshy tables of the heart (2 Corinthians 3:1-3).

Of his own will begat he us with the word of truth, that we should be a kind of firstfruits of his creatures. (James 1:18).

STOP CASTING ALL OF YOUR CARES ONTO FACEBOOK:

CALL 1-800-JESUS!

Humble yourselves therefore under the mighty hand of God, that he may exalt you in due time: Casting all your care upon him; for he careth for you (1 Peter 5:6-7).

Cast thy burden upon the LORD, and he shall sustain thee: he shall never suffer the righteous to be moved (Psalm 55:22).

But he giveth more grace. Wherefore he saith, God resisteth the proud, but giveth grace unto the humble (James 4:6).

THE GREATEST GIFT I HAVE EVER RECEIVED IS ETERNAL LIFE!

For the wages of sin is death; but the gift of God is eternal life through Jesus Christ our Lord (Romans 6:23).

And I saw no temple therein: for the Lord God Almighty and the Lamb are the temple of it. And the city had no need of the sun, neither of the moon, to shine in it: for the glory of God did lighten it, and the Lamb is the light thereof. And the nations of them which are saved shall walk in the light of it: and the kings of the earth do bring their glory and honour into it. And the gates of it shall not be shut at all by day: for there shall be no night there. And they shall bring the glory and honour of the nations into it. And there shall in no wise enter into it anything that defileth, neither whatsoever worketh abomination, or maketh a lie: but they which are written in the Lamb's book of life (Revelation 21:22-27).

INDEPENDENCE DAY REALLY TOOK PLACE AT CALVARY!

But we speak the wisdom of God in a mystery, even the hidden wisdom, which God ordained before the world unto our glory: Which none of the princes of this world knew: for had they known it, they would not have crucified the Lord of glory (1 Corinthians 2:7-8).

And having spoiled principalities and powers, he made a shew of them openly, triumphing over them in it (Colossians 2:15).

Who was delivered for our offences, and was raised again for our justification (Romans 4:25).

If the Son therefore shall make you free, ye shall be free indeed (John 8:36).

NO OTHER WATER CAN CLEANSE YOU LIKE THE WATER OF GOD'S WORD: IT'S FROM THE INSIDE OUT!

That he might sanctify and cleanse it with the washing of water by the word. That he might present it to himself a glorious church, not having spot, or wrinkle, or any such thing; but that it should be holy and without blemish. (Ephesians 5:26-27).

Now ye are clean through the word which I have spoken unto you (John 15:3).

WE MUST LIVE EACH DAY ANTICIPATING THE LORD'S RETURN!

Behold, I come as a thief. Blessed *is* he that watcheth, and keepeth his garments, lest he walk naked, and they see his shame (Revelation 16:15).

But ye, brethren, are not in darkness, that that day should overtake you as a thief (1 Thessalonians 5:4).

NEVER RESPOND TO A NAME YOU'RE NOT: ONLY RESPOND TO WHO GOD SAID YOU ARE!

For whom he did foreknow, he also did predestinate to be conformed to the image of his Son, that he might be the firstborn among many brethren. Moreover whom he did predestinate, them he also called: and whom he called, them he also justified: and whom he justified, them he also glorified (Romans 8:29-30).

IF I NEVER RECEIVE A ROSE GARDEN IN THIS LIFE, THAT'S ALL RIGHT! I HAVE JESUS THAT SWEET SMELLING SAVOUR, THAT SACRIFICE THAT'S WELL PLEASING UNTO GOD:

I am the rose of Sharon, and the lily of the valleys (Song of Solomon 2:1).

And walk in love, as Christ also hath loved us, and hath given himself for us an offering and a sacrifice to God for a sweetsmelling savour (Ephesians 5:2).

For we are unto God a sweet savour of Christ, in them that are saved, and in them that perish (2 Corinthians 2:15).

I am Alpha and Omega, the beginning and the ending, saith the Lord, which is, and which was, and which is to come, the Almighty (Revelation 1:8).

INSPIRED WORDS OF EDIFICATION

MEDITATION REFLECTION JOURNAL

Let the words of my mouth, and the meditation of my heart, be acceptable in thy sight, O LORD, my strength, and my redeemer (Psalm 19:14).

_____
_____
_____
_____
_____
_____
_____
_____
_____
_____
_____
_____
_____
_____
_____
_____
_____
_____
_____
_____
_____
_____
_____
_____

INSPIRED WORDS OF EDIFICATION

INSPIRED WORDS OF EDIFICATION

ISBN-13: 978-0692044162 Copyright @ 2018 Word of Reconciliation Restoration Outreach Ministries Inc.

ISBN-10: 0692044167

Websites:

Word of Reconciliation Restoration Outreach Ministries Inc.

www.wordofrest.org

pastorfloraskipwith@gmail.com

Flora M Skipwith Nations Ministries Inc.

www.fmskipwithnationsministries.com

fmskipwithnations@gmail.com

P. O. Box 2564

Chester, VA 23831-9998

(804) 318-3084

Founders:

Bishop Dexter T Skipwith

Senior Pastor Flora M Skipwith

INSPIRED WORDS OF EDIFICATION

TO REQUEST THE AUTHOR FOR SPEAKING ENGAGEMENTS

VISIT WEBSITE:

www.fmskipwithnationsministries.com

fmskipwithnations@gmail.com

I pray now in the name of Jesus Christ that the Lord will bless you richly for your liberal giving into the ministry through purchasing this book. Your financial contributions will be used solely towards the work of the ministry!

Your Servant In Christ,

Pastor Flora Skipwith

www.ingramcontent.com/pod-product-compliance
Lightning Source LLC
Chambersburg PA
CBHW031213090426
42736CB00009B/893